MAGIC OF

*How Earthing Helps to Heal Your
Body, Harnessing the Healing Power of
Nature and Effective Grounding
Techniques to Achieve Instant Calm*

Dani Twain

Copyright Notice

All rights reserved. No part of this publication may be reproduced, stored in a retrieval system or transmitted in any form or by any means, including electronic, digital, mechanical, photocopying, audio recording, printing or otherwise, without written permission from the publisher or the author.

Contents

COPYRIGHT

INTRODUCTION

Chapter One

Modern People Are Disconnected from the Earth

The Earth is a Huge Electric Pile

The Electrical Interaction Between the Earth and the Human Body

Chapter 2

What is Grounding

The Earth as a Gigantic Battery

We have lost contact with the ground

13 Signs You're Not Grounded

Chapter 3

The Health Benefits of Grounding

- Reduce inflammation
- Grounding to Counter Chronic Inflammation

- Earthing Has Profound Implications for Physical Health
- Grounding for Instant Stress or Anxiety Relief

Other Body Benefits of Grounding.

Chapter 4

Earthing Theory: Why It Works

Ground Yourself in Your Bioelectrical Body

The Electromagnetic Earth

Chapter 5

How to Ground Yourself: 15 Grounding Techniques

Chapter 6

How to Ground Yourself Indoors (Electrically)

Chapter 7

The Best Grounding Tools and Techniques

Chapter 8

Maximize the Effectiveness of Grounding Techniques and Earthing

Chapter 9

Forest bathing

Chapter 10

My own experience with grounding

Grounding for you

Recap: How to Ground Yourself

Introduction

This Guide will explain the science and benefits of grounding and earthing, as well as how you can ground yourself using various methods.

Imagine you are walking barefoot on the beach.

Feel the warm sun on your skin.

Listen to the sound of the waves crashing.

Smell the salty ocean breeze as it blows past you.

Now, pay attention to your feet. Do they tingle? Do you feel warmth spreading through your body?

You might have felt something similar when walking barefoot on grass.

At those times, you are grounded. This is one reason why many people love going to the beach.

Luckily, there are grounding techniques that can help you feel the same way. These techniques can help you reduce anxiety, clear your mind, recharge your body, and calm yourself.

Let's explore ...

Chapter 1

Modern People Are Disconnected from the Earth

Today, we are disconnected from the earth, not just in a philosophical or pecological way, but also in an electrical way. People living in cities are far from nature, but the main issue is our lost electrical connection to the earth.

Nowadays, we spend most of our time electrically isolated from the ground. This is mainly because of the shoes we wear, our daily activities, and the homes we live in.

Modern shoes with rubber soles insulate us from the earth, while in the past, people walked barefoot or with leather soles that didn't block the electrical connection. Agricultural work used to ensure daily skin contact with the earth, but now, most jobs don't involve direct contact with the ground. Long ago, people slept on the ground or on floors made of earth or stone, which maintained this electrical connection, unlike today's houses and beds made with insulating materials.

By losing this electrical connection, modern people miss out on several benefits.

The Earth is a Huge Electric Battery

The earth works like a big electric battery, constantly recharged by sunlight, lightning, and the heat from its core. The earth's surface is an endless source of free electrons, which are tiny particles with negative charges. These electrons move to balance out positive charges, similar to how electricity flows through a wire.

The Electrical Interaction Between the Earth and the Human Body

Our bodies are full of complex electrical circuits. Everything our body does, from moving nutrients and water in cells to the brain, heart, muscles, and immune system, relies on electrical energy.

When we are in direct contact with the earth, our bodies can benefit from these electrical charges and rhythms, helping our different functions stay balanced. The earth's electrical signals also help set our biological cycles correctly.

Chapter 2

What is Grounding?

Grounding, also known as earthing, can mean two things:
1. Becoming fully present in your body.
2. Electrically connecting yourself to the earth.

We've all felt grounded at some point—those moments when we feel "at home" in our bodies, less anxious, more focused, and calm.

Grounding techniques are methods and exercises that help us achieve this state. These techniques can be physical, mental, emotional, or energetic.

The Earth as a Gigantic Battery

The earth acts like a giant battery, containing a natural, subtle electrical charge. This special kind of energy exists in the ground and gives us a sense of security and stability.

Scientific research has shown that direct physical contact with the earth's surface, which is full of electrons, can have positive effects on our health. This connection is important because our bodies, made mostly of water and minerals, are good conductors of electricity.

Unfortunately, modern lifestyles often separate us from this contact with the earth. Studies suggest that this lack of connection might contribute to physical and mental health problems.

Benefits of Reconnecting with the Earth

Research has found that reconnecting with the earth's electrons can lead to amazing physiological changes and improved well-being. Grounding can help improve sleep and reduce pain. This can be done by walking barefoot outdoors or using conductive systems indoors, like special sheets or mats that transfer the earth's electrons to our bodies.

Our bodies constantly produce and use electrical energy. When we receive extra electrons from the earth, our bodies can clean, repair, and function more efficiently.

Grounding is a simple way to reconnect with the earth and support our health and well-being.

We Have Lost Contact with the Ground

You are a bioelectric being living on an electric planet. All your cells send out multiple frequencies that control your heart, immune system, muscles, and nervous system.

Except for humans in industrial societies, all living things on our planet stay connected to the earth's electrical energy.

Unlike other creatures, we rarely go barefoot outside. For many decades, we have worn shoes with rubber and plastic soles that block the earth's energy and keep us from making electrical contact with the ground.

We also don't sleep on the floor anymore, as many cultures did in the past. Many of us work in high-rise buildings far above the ground.

The truth is, we are disconnected and ungrounded—out of touch with the earth.

13 Signs You're Not Grounded

How can you tell if you're grounded or not? Here are some signs that you might be ungrounded:

Mental and Emotional Signs

- You get distracted easily.
- You often space out.
- You overthink or constantly ruminate.
- You get caught up in personal drama.
- You experience constant anxiety and worry.

Behavioral Signs

- You're obsessed with your personal image.
- You have a strong desire for material things, like brands.
- You are easily deceived by yourself or others.

Physical Signs

- You have inflammation.
- You experience poor sleep.
- You suffer from chronic pain.
- You feel fatigued.
- You have poor circulation.

Being ungrounded is a widespread issue. This problem is so common that many people don't even realize it exists.

Chapter 3

The Health Benefits of Grounding

Reducing Inflammation

Grounding allows your body to absorb free electrons from the earth, which can neutralize harmful reactive oxygen species, also known as free radicals. This process acts like antioxidants and helps reduce both acute and chronic inflammation. Grounding has been shown to reduce signs of inflammation following an injury, such as redness, heat, swelling, pain, and loss of function. It is also believed that grounding can prevent or reduce "silent," chronic inflammation in the body, which is a known cause of many chronic diseases.

Improving Sleep

Connecting your body to the earth while sleeping can help normalize your cortisol levels, also known as the "stress hormone." In one study, participants used a grounding device while they slept for 8 weeks. This device involved a conductive bedsheet connected to a grounding rod outside. Participants reported improved sleep quality, reduced pain, and lower stress levels after the 8 weeks.

Reducing Pain and Muscle Damage

A study on muscle damage from exercise (specifically 200 half squats) showed that grounding can help reduce muscle damage. Participants who were grounded for 4 hours after the exercise, both on the day of the exercise and the day after, showed significantly reduced levels of creatine kinase (CK), a marker of muscle damage. This indicates that grounding helped reduce muscle damage. Grounding is already used in sports to speed up muscle recovery and wound healing after intense exercise, such as during the Tour de France cycling race.

Improving Mood

In a double-blind study with 40 adults, one group was grounded while the other group thought they were grounded but were not. The grounded group showed statistically significant improvements in mood compared to the sham-grounded group. This indicates that grounding can improve mood beyond just providing relaxation.

Reducing Blood Viscosity (Thinning the Blood)

One study showed that grounding for 2 hours increased the surface charge of red blood cells, which reduces blood viscosity and prevents red blood cells from sticking together. Thick blood is a risk factor for cardiovascular disease, so the study suggests that grounding could be a simple way to reduce the risk of cardiovascular events.

Reducing Stress and Promoting Relaxation

The sympathetic nervous system helps you switch into "fight mode" during danger or stress. Its opposite, the parasympathetic nervous system, activates when you feel relaxed and safe. Nowadays, our sympathetic nervous system is often overactive due to stressful lives, so it's important to find ways to activate the parasympathetic nervous system. Many people use relaxation techniques, meditation, or exercise to achieve this. Grounding could be another helpful strategy.

In a double-blind study, participants were either grounded for 2 hours or were not grounded (sham grounded). The researchers found several effects of grounding:
1. An immediate decrease in skin conductivity during grounding and an increase after.
2. An increase in respiratory rate.
3. Stabilization of blood oxygen levels.
4. An increase in pulse frequency variance.

The immediate decrease in skin conductivity shows quick activation of the parasympathetic nervous system and deactivation of the sympathetic nervous system. The other changes suggest the start of a healing response that needs more oxygen.

Heart rate variability (HRV) measures the variation between heartbeats and is controlled by the autonomic nervous system. Low HRV is linked to stress, depression, anxiety, and a higher risk of heart disease. High HRV is associated with relaxation. Activities like meditation, sleep, and physical exercise can increase HRV. Grounding can also help increase HRV.

In another double-blind study, participants alternated between being grounded for 2 hours and having sham grounding sessions without knowing which was which. The study showed a significant increase in HRV during the grounded sessions. Since improved HRV is a good sign for heart health, researchers suggested that grounding could help support the cardiovascular system.

Grounding to Counter Chronic Inflammation

One major benefit of grounding is that it provides the body with an unlimited supply of free electrons. These free electrons can neutralize positive charges in the body that cause chronic inflammation. During inflammation, free radicals are formed. Free radicals are unstable molecules missing an electron, and they can damage cell molecules like DNA by stealing electrons, causing a chain reaction of damage.

Antioxidants from food help counteract free radicals, but sometimes they aren't enough. Grounding acts as a powerful antioxidant by supplying free electrons to neutralize free radicals, which can reduce chronic inflammation and related diseases.

A study used thermography, or infrared imaging, to evaluate grounding's impact on inflammation. Thermography measures surface temperature and shows warmer areas in red and cooler areas in blue. Inflammation appears as red areas. The study compared thermographic images taken before and after 30 minutes of grounding and observed significant changes.

Earthing and Physical Health

Research shows that earthing can help heal a variety of ailments naturally. Cyclists in the Tour de France often suffer from illnesses, tendonitis, and poor sleep due to extreme physical and mental stress. The American team tried earthing after their daily competitions and reported better sleep, fewer illnesses, no tendonitis, and faster recovery.

From my experience, the benefits of earthing extend beyond physical health. It also has mental and emotional benefits that support psychological well-being and peak experiences.

Grounding for Instant Stress or Anxiety Relief

When you face a stressful or dangerous situation, your mind and body naturally react with the fight-or-flight response. This is useful for reacting quickly to danger, but sometimes it can overreact, leaving you frozen or detached and unable to think clearly. Anxiety disorders or prolonged reactions to trauma can cause unnecessary hyperactive reactions, interfering with daily life and leaving you exhausted. Anxiety can also create a cycle where initial stress leads to more anxiety or panic.

Grounding techniques help distract you from unwanted thoughts and control anxious reactions. They can help you move out of a frozen state, think more clearly, and choose how to act. Grounding can break the cycle of anxiety, giving you a greater sense of control and confidence.

Grounding Techniques to Try

When anxiety becomes overwhelming, try these grounding techniques. Experiment with one, two, or more until you find what works for you.

Physical and Sensory Grounding Methods

1. Feet on the Ground: Place both feet on the floor or ground. Stomp them a few times, shift your weight from one foot to the other, or wiggle your toes, focusing on the sensations in your feet and ankles.

2. Hands Together: Press or rub your palms together, noticing the pressure, temperature, and how it feels.

3. Touch an Object: Find a small object within reach. Pay attention to its texture, weight, and whether it is warm or cool.

4. Finger Tapping: Tap your fingers on your knees. Notice the sensation in your fingers and knees, and the rhythm you create. Try alternating between left and right taps.

5. Water Sensations: Place your hands in water, focusing on how it feels on different parts of your hands.

6. Ice Holding: Hold a piece of ice in your hand, noticing the cold sensation and how it feels as it melts.

7. Cold Water Face Splash: Soak your face in cold water for a few seconds or splash cold water on your face. The cool temperature on your skin can help break the anxiety spiral.

8. Deep Breathing: Breathe deeply and slowly. Place your hand on your stomach and feel it move with each breath.

9. Taste and Smell: Enjoy the taste of food or drink in your mouth, or the aroma of a spice, herb, or soap.

10. Listening: Listen to the sounds around you, whether it's traffic, birds, wind, or any other noise. Identify the sounds and let them remind you of your surroundings.

11. Movement: Get moving by stretching, jumping up and down, walking, or jogging (even if it's just in place). Notice how your body feels as you move and the sensation when your feet touch the ground.

These grounding techniques can help you regain control and reduce anxiety, allowing you to feel more at ease and present in the moment.

Mental Grounding Techniques

Focusing on a mental task can help you break free from an anxiety reaction. Here are some techniques to try:

1. Family Names: Name each member of your family, their age, and what makes each one special.

2. Detailed Colors: Look at an object and name its color as accurately as possible, using specific shades like burgundy, raspberry, turquoise, or navy blue.

3. Memory Game: Play a memory game by recalling as many details as you can about a familiar place or looking closely at a photograph, then turning it face down and trying to recreate it in your mind with as much detail as possible.

4. Counting Backwards: Count back from 100. Start with ones, then try sevens or other intervals.

5. Writing Backwards: Write your name or the names of people you know backwards.

6. Reciting: Recite a poem, passage from a book, or the lyrics to a favorite song aloud.

7. Describing Actions: Think of a simple action and describe each step it involves.

8. Categorizing: Pick a category, such as animals, sports teams, rivers, or vegetables, and name as many things in that category as you can in a minute or two.

Calming Grounding Techniques

Here are some calming techniques to help soothe anxiety:

1. Imagining Faces: Picture the face of someone you care about or imagine their voice and what they might say to reassure you.
2. Favorite Place: Remember your favorite place—what it looks like, its sounds and smells, and how you would feel if you were there.
3. Soothing Touch: Touch something soothing, like a soft or smooth fabric on your bedding or clothing.

4. Pet Time: Spend a few quiet moments with your pet or imagine what it would be like to sit with them.

5. Asking for Help: Don't hesitate to ask for help.

Seeking Professional Help

A professional counselor can help you find strategies to combat anxiety, including how to use these grounding and calming techniques. They can also help you identify the background and triggers of your anxiety and guide you toward effective treatment.

Other Body Benefits of Grounding

Grounding the human body has shown several benefits in the limited studies conducted on the subject. Here are some of the benefits outlined in the book:

1. Reduction of Chronic Pain: Grounding may reduce or eliminate chronic pain.

2. Improved Sleep: Grounding has been linked to better sleep quality.

3. Increased Energy: Some people report feeling more energized after grounding.

4. Stress Reduction: Grounding has been found to reduce levels of the stress hormone cortisol in the blood, leading to lower stress levels.

5. Blood Thinning: Grounding may thin the blood, which can lower blood pressure and improve circulation.

6. Muscle Relaxation: Grounding has been shown to reduce muscle tension and alleviate headaches.

7. Menstrual Symptom Relief: Some women experience relief from menstrual symptoms through grounding.

8. Wound Healing: Grounding may accelerate wound healing and help prevent bed sores.

9. Jet Lag Reduction: Grounding could reduce or eliminate the effects of jet lag.

10. Electromagnetic Wave Protection: Grounding may protect the body from potential harmful effects of electromagnetic waves.

11. Faster Recovery: Grounding has been observed to speed up recovery after intense physical activity.

These benefits suggest that grounding may have positive effects on various aspects of health and well-being, although more research is needed to fully understand its mechanisms and effectiveness.

Chapter 4

Earthing Theory: Why It Works

The idea behind earthing is simple: when we connect with the Earth, we absorb negatively charged electrons from its surface into our bodies.

These electrons help neutralize positively charged free radicals that cause chronic inflammation—a condition where our body's defense system goes into overdrive, damaging cell membranes and DNA, which can lead to diseases like cancer.

Studies suggest that earthing can reduce blood thickness and inflammation, which might help support our heart health.

Many of us live with an overactive sympathetic nervous system due to emotional stress. Early research indicates that earthing can have a calming effect on this system, helping to balance it out.

Biophysicist James Oschman explains that as soon as we touch the Earth or connect to it through a wire, our body's functions start to normalize. It's like flipping a switch that turns on our body's anti-inflammatory response. When we don't connect with the Earth, we miss out on these free electrons that can help fight disease and protect our cells from damage.

Earthing is described as one of the simplest and most impactful lifestyle changes we can make for our health.

Ground Yourself in Your Bioelectrical Body

Humans are filled with electromagnetic energy. Inside and around us, there are electrical currents and magnetic fields that control how our body works.

This network of energy fields, known as the human biofield in energy medicine, is crucial for our health. In ancient healing traditions like Ayurvedic medicine from India and Chinese medicine, this energy is called prana or qi. It's believed to be the life force flowing through us, affecting our physical, mental, and emotional well-being.

When this energy flow is blocked or out of balance, it can lead to illness. Modern therapies like Reiki also work on the idea of balancing this energy.

The Electromagnetic Earth

In Chinese belief, our body's energy, or qi, comes from two sources: Heavenly Qi and Earth Qi.

Heavenly Qi comes from the sun and the wider cosmos.

Earth Qi, on the other hand, comes from the Earth itself—the natural energy web, magnetic fields, and heat it generates.

Interestingly, the Earth has its own energetic system similar to ours. It has energy centers, channels, and magnetic fields, similar to what we have in our bodies. This idea of interconnectedness is reflected in the saying "As above, so below."

The Earth acts like a giant battery, constantly recharged by solar radiation and lightning. Every minute, around 5,000 lightning strikes somewhere on Earth, adding to this natural energy.

Earthing, or grounding, taps into this powerful natural energy source, helping us connect with the Earth's energy for our well-being.

Chapter 5

How to Ground Yourself: 15 Grounding Techniques

To make the most of these grounding techniques, it's important to pay attention to how you feel during and after using them. This helps reinforce the positive effects and encourages you to use them again in the future.

Grounding Yourself Outside: Stand Barefoot

Connecting with the Earth is simple: just kick off your shoes and socks and step outside!

Walking barefoot might seem old-fashioned in today's world, but it's how our ancestors moved around instinctively.

Find a spot with natural ground like grass, sand, or dirt. You can stand still, take a stroll, or even lie down.

Just like in an electrical circuit, you only need one point of contact with the ground to establish a connection. While one foot is enough, I've found that having both feet on the ground feels more powerful.

For healing benefits, experts suggest spending at least 20 minutes barefoot on the Earth, twice a day. But even a short 10-minute walk during your lunch break can be beneficial.

Remember:
- Avoid grass treated with pesticides.
- Watch out for sharp objects like broken glass.
- Avoid walking barefoot on hot asphalt.
- If going barefoot isn't possible, try earthing shoes.

Time: 20 minutes.

Take a Cold Shower

Cold showers offer numerous health benefits and were made famous by Wim Hof.

Cold exposure can:
- Boost immunity
- Aid in weight loss
- Improve mood by triggering dopamine release

If you're new to cold showers, start by making the water warm/cool for 30 seconds at the end of your regular shower. Gradually decrease the temperature over three weeks while increasing the duration.

By the end of the three weeks, your body will adapt to the cold. It's an energizing and grounding experience.

Focus the cold water on the back of your neck and the top of your head for maximum effect.

Note: Avoid cold showers if you have high blood pressure.

Time: 30 seconds to 5 minutes.

Observe Your Breath

Mindful breathing is a classic way to ground yourself and find calm.

Here's how:

1. Close your eyes and turn your focus inward.
2. Let your awareness sink into your body.
3. Take a moment to observe your breath—how your body naturally inhales and exhales.

Don't try to change or control your breath. Just witness the natural rhythm of your breath as it happens on its own.

In Eastern traditions, this method is often called "tuning the breath" or simply focusing on your breath.

The more you practice, the better it works. The key is to observe without trying to force any changes. Let your body lead the way, and your mind will follow.

Time: 1 to 10 minutes.

Feel Your Feet

This technique is quick and effective, perfect for calming down in the moment.

Here's how:

1. Sit or stand comfortably.

2. Focus all your attention on the bottom of your feet.

3. Notice any sensations you feel there.

It might take a few minutes to start feeling anything, especially if you're feeling very unsettled. Starting with mindful breathing can help make this technique even more effective.

Time: 30 seconds to 5 minutes.

Stand Like a Tree

This method helps you feel grounded and stable, like a tree firmly rooted in the earth. Here's how:

1. Stand with your feet shoulder-width apart and parallel.

2. Keep your head lifted, chin slightly tucked, and shoulders relaxed.

3. Let your hands rest at your sides or place them over your navel.

4. Allow your body's weight to sink downward, without slouching.

5. If possible, imagine roots growing from the soles of your feet, reaching deep into the earth.

6. For added benefits, try this technique outdoors, preferably barefoot on the earth.

This practice is a simplified version of an ancient standing meditation called Zhan Zhuang.

Time: 5 to 10 minutes.

Cover Your Crown

In Chinese medicine and energy practices, there's a special point at the top of your head called Baihui. It's like the center point of your crown.

When you're feeling all over the place, just put one hand gently over the top of your head. That's it. If you want, close your eyes to focus better.

Time: 30 seconds to 1 minute.

Eat Grounding Foods

Did you know that some foods can help you feel more grounded?

These are some grounding foods:
- Meats

- Root veggies like sweet potatoes, carrots, and beets
- Winter squashes like acorn and butternut

Just eating these foods can make you feel more grounded. Sometimes, a warm sweet potato can really do the trick.

Mindful Walking (Barefoot or with Shoes)

Walking can help you feel more centered, especially if you do it mindfully.

My favorite way to ground myself is by walking barefoot outside. It only takes a few minutes for my mind to calm down.

Walking barefoot also massages special points on your feet, like Kidney-1 or "bubbling well."

But even if you wear shoes, you can still ground yourself while walking. Just keep your focus on the present moment. Watch your thoughts without getting caught up in them.

Time: 10 to 20 minutes.

Roll Around Like a Cat

Have you ever noticed how cats and some dogs love rolling around on the ground?

It seems like they know something we don't—they're releasing negative energy!

Try it yourself. Roll around on the ground, get a little dirty. You'll see why cats enjoy it so much. It feels great!

Time: However long you want.

Spend More Time in Nature

Being in nature is like hitting the reset button for our minds.

When we're cooped up indoors too much, it's a sign we're not grounded.

But you don't need any special tricks to reconnect with nature. Just make an effort to spend less time inside and more time outside.

Even if you live in a busy city, find a park or green space to unwind. In places like New York City, you've got Central Park nearby.

Nature can help balance out all the screen time we get. So, try to spend at least 30 minutes to a whole day outside—it really works!

Time: 30 minutes to all day long.

Earthing Visualization

Sit or stand comfortably and close your eyes.

Feel the ground supporting you and take a deep breath.

Focus on your heart. Imagine a warm energy radiating from it.

Now, picture the center of the Earth—maybe it's a glowing core or a circle of light.

Visualize a beam of energy connecting your heart to the Earth's core, forming a loop.

Feel the connection between your heart and the Earth.

Time: 2 to 5 minutes.

Mindful Stretching

Stretching can be more than just a physical exercise—it can also help ground your mind and body.

If you already have a stretching routine from yoga, qigong, or elsewhere, that's perfect. Or you can find one on Youtube.

The key to mindful stretching is to stay present. Instead of letting your mind wander, focus on the sensation of stretching and how your body feels.

This helps integrate your body and mind, making it a great way to ground yourself, especially before meditation.

Time: 5 to 10 minutes.

Mindful Body Scan

Sit, stand, or lie down comfortably with your eyes closed.

Start by taking a few deep breaths to settle your mind.

Then, imagine yourself floating in a small boat, gently drifting down a river.

Begin at the top of your head and slowly scan down through your body, noticing any sensations you feel.

Move down through your neck, shoulders, arms, chest, torso, hips, legs, and feet.

A body scan can help you feel more settled and grounded.

Time: 5 – 20 minutes.

54321 Method

This method helps you ground yourself by focusing on your physical senses.

Start by looking around and noticing five things you can see.

Then, pay attention to four things you can touch, whether it's your clothes, furniture, or the ground beneath your feet.

Next, listen for three things you can hear around you. Focus on sounds, not your thoughts.

After that, try to smell two distinct scents in your environment.

Finally, notice one thing you can taste. Maybe it's the lingering flavor of your breakfast or the toothpaste you used this morning.

Repeat this process as many times as you like to help bring yourself into the present moment.

Time: As long as it takes.

Grounding Yourself Indoors (Electrically)

In our modern homes, we're surrounded by electronic devices like smartphones, computers, and Wi-Fi routers, which emit electromagnetic radiation (EMF). Learning how to ground ourselves indoors can help counteract the harmful effects of this radiation.

Here are some ways to ground yourself indoors:

- Wall Outlet Grounding: If your house is wired with a ground (copper rod), you can lightly touch the center screw in a wall electrical outlet to ground yourself.

- Radiator or Copper Pipe: Touching a radiator or a copper pipe can also help you ground yourself electrically.

- Grounding Mat: Using a grounding mat is another option. These mats are made of conductive material and are plugged into any electric outlet's grounding port. As long as your skin is in contact with the mat, you are technically grounded.

- Concrete Basement: If you have a concrete basement, standing barefoot on the floor can help ground you as well.

Grounding Yourself When Using a PC

It's important to stay electrically grounded when working in front of a computer or any electronic device. Here's how:

- Earthing Pads: Earthing pads are made of conductive material and are plugged into the grounding port of an electric outlet. Your skin needs to be in contact with the pad to be grounded. You can either purchase a universal earthing mat or make your own using materials like copper mesh and a grounding plug.

How to Ground Yourself Using Earthing Products

If you're unable to ground yourself outdoors, earthing products can be a convenient alternative. These products, like earthing pads, allow you to connect to the Earth's natural energy while indoors. They can be particularly useful during colder months when walking barefoot outside isn't feasible.

Time: Whenever you're using electronic devices or feel the need to ground yourself indoors.

The Earthing Movement and Its Products

The Earthing movement has led to the creation of various products aimed at grounding individuals by connecting them to the Earth's natural energy through their home's ground wire.

These products include:

- Earthing bed sheets
- Pillow covers
- Grounding mats for desks
- Chair mats
- Patches
- Earthing shoes

While these products claim to offer benefits, such as reducing stress and improving sleep, some suggest that the positive effects reported could be due to the placebo effect—a psychological phenomenon where belief in a treatment leads to perceived improvements.

Can Earthing Products Make a Difference?

It's uncertain whether these products truly provide health benefits, but early research suggests they might. For some users, like myself, earthing shoes don't quite replicate the feeling of being barefoot, but they still offer a grounding effect.

Even without these products, you can ground yourself at home. Surfaces like ceramic tile and concrete flooring can ground you if you walk barefoot. However, materials like carpet, vinyl, and wood flooring won't have the same effect.

Personal Experience with Earthing Products

After using earthing pads and sheets for years, I find the principle behind earthing promising. However, aside from earthing shoes, I haven't noticed significant effects from these products. This doesn't mean they don't work, but rather that individual experiences may vary. For some, optimizing sleep alongside using earthing sheets might lead to noticeable benefits, as reported by many users.

Chapter 7

Grounding Techniques for Anxiety

These grounding techniques can help when you're feeling anxious. With practice, they become easier and can be used whenever you need to calm down.

1. Engage Your Senses:
Close your eyes and take slow, deep breaths. Focus on your breathing to relax.

Then, open your eyes and ask yourself:
- What do I see?
- What do I feel?

- What do I hear?
- What do I smell?
- What do I taste?

Stay in the moment and pay attention to each sense. Take a few more deep breaths when you're done.

2. Hold an Object:
Find a small object like a smooth stone or paperweight.

Hold it in your hand and focus on its details. Notice its color, texture, and weight.

Reflect on how it feels in your hand. Is it smooth, rough, heavy, or light?

Spend some time with the object, fully present and grounded in the moment.

3. Grounding Chair:

Simply sitting down can help us feel grounded, no matter where we are.

Focus on the feeling of sitting in your chair, the weight of your body against it, and the texture of the material.

Next, press your feet firmly into the ground. Imagine any heaviness in your mind and body flowing down into the ground, leaving you feeling lighter.

Take a few slow breaths and when you're ready, bring your attention back to the room. Notice how you feel more present and less burdened.

4. Self-Reflective Questions:

Anxiety can sometimes make us feel disconnected from reality. Asking yourself questions can bring you back to the present moment.

Take a moment to answer these questions:

- Where am I right now?
- What day and month is it?
- What season is it?
- How old am I?
- Where do I live, and with whom?

Think about how your ancestors have led you to this moment.

5. Positive Coping Statement:

Prepare a statement to help you cope when anxiety arises.

For example:
"My name is X. Everything happening now will pass. There will come a time when I can look back on this without fear."

Repeat this statement, focusing on each word, and remember that difficult times are temporary.

Grounding Technique: Three-Minute Breathing Space Meditation

Mindful breathing can be a great way to ground yourself in the present moment.

Here's a simple three-minute breathing space meditation, recommended by Williams and Penman (2016), to help you feel more centered:

1. Explore Your Experience:

- Sit comfortably with your back straight and close your eyes.

- Notice what thoughts are passing through your mind. Just observe them without trying to change them.

- Acknowledge any feelings present, whether they're positive or negative.

- Pay attention to any bodily sensations, like tightness or discomfort. Allow them to be there without trying to alter them.

2. Gather and Focus:

- Imagine a spotlight shining on the physical sensations of each breath.

- Zoom in on the sensation of your breath in your abdomen. You can place your hand on your stomach to help focus.

- Keep your attention on the sensation of your breath as it expands and contracts.

3. Expand Your Attention:

- Expand your awareness to include your entire body as you continue to breathe.

- Notice any discomfort or tension in your body, allowing each breath to move around these sensations.

- Instead of trying to change them, accept and befriend these sensations.

4. Conclusion:

- When you're ready, take a few deep breaths and gently open your eyes.

- Return your focus to your surroundings while carrying the sense of calmness with you.

Practice this meditation whenever you need to ground yourself and find peace in the present moment.

Grounding Technique: Finger and Shape Breathing for Children

When children feel anxious and their breath becomes short and shallow, mastering their breathing can help them regain control and calmness.

Here's a simple exercise that children can do either alone or in a group to manage their anxiety:

1. Follow the Hand:

- Ask the child to hold up one hand with the fingers spread out.

- With their eyes open or closed, have them gently trace the outline of their hand using their gaze or another finger.

- As they trace up each finger, they should take a slow and deep breath in.

- Then, as they trace down the other side of the finger, they should exhale slowly.

- Repeat this process for each finger on the hand, breathing in as they go up and breathing out as they go down.

2. Repeat and Practice:

- Encourage the child to repeat this exercise for all five fingers on one hand.

- If they wish to continue, they can repeat the process for the other hand as well.

- Remind them to practice this exercise regularly so they can use it whenever they start to feel anxious.

This simple breathing technique helps children focus their attention on their breath and brings a sense of calmness and control, helping them manage their anxiety effectively.

Chapter 8

Enhancing Grounding Techniques and Earthing

To make grounding and earthing techniques more effective, it's crucial to consciously connect with your body and the Earth.

The more time spent using electronic devices like computers and phones, the greater the benefits of grounding and earthing become.

While some argue that electromagnetic frequencies (EMF) and radiation from devices aren't harmful, evidence suggests otherwise.

Ultimately, experiencing the effects of EMF radiation in your energetic body dispels any doubts.

It's not a matter of whether these waves affect you but rather to what extent you feel their impact.

Regardless, grounding in your body and daily earthing practices can contribute to a long and vibrant life.

Learning practices like qigong or The Mastery Method can help you become more attuned to the energy within your body.

Chapter 9

Forest Bathing

What is Forest Bathing?

Forest bathing is a therapeutic practice rooted in spending time in nature, particularly under the shelter of trees. Originating in Japan, forest therapy is becoming increasingly popular among those interested in nurturing their mental well-being and establishing a deeper bond with the natural world. Let's delve into what forest bathing entails and why it's an activity worth trying for its health benefits.

Understanding Forest Bathing

Contrary to what the name suggests, forest bathing doesn't involve actually taking a bath in the forest. Instead, it's about embracing your surroundings and immersing yourself in nature's embrace.

When you forest bathe, you enter the woods to experience its tranquil ambiance, listen to the calming sounds of nature, observe the serene scenery of organic life, breathe in the fresh air, and let go of stress as you become one with the forest environment.

Essentially, forest bathing involves strolling through the woods with no specific destination in mind. It's about being present in the moment, fully absorbing the forest atmosphere, and embracing mindfulness. It serves as a form of ecotherapy and a method of stress relief, offering potential benefits for immune system function as well.

Origins of Forest Bathing

The practice of forest bathing, known as "Shinrin Yoku" in Japanese, was introduced by the Japan Forestry Agency in 1982. "Shinrin" translates to forest, and "Yoku" means bath or bathing. It emerged as a response to the high levels of depression in Japanese society and the adverse effects of excessive technology use, which led to people spending less time outdoors. Recognizing the healing power of nature, the Japanese ministry advocated for spending time in forests as a means to promote a healthier lifestyle. Since then, forest bathing has gained global recognition and popularity.

Benefits of Nature Walks

Scientific research highlights a multitude of benefits associated with spending time in nature. Forest walks not only improve mental health but also provide an opportunity for physical activity.

Benefits of Spending Time in Nature

Exploring the woods and indulging in nature walks offer specific advantages that can enhance your overall well-being:

1. Relaxation: Walking in nature provides an opportunity to experience peace, quiet, and solitude, triggering a relaxation response in your body.

2. Fresh Air: City pollution can irritate your lungs, but nature walks offer a breath of

fresh air. Deep breathing amid the trees can refresh your lungs and serve as a reset.

3. Technology Break: Disconnect from constant technology and information overload. Nature's beauty can help you reconnect with the Earth.

4. Connection with Nature: Engage your senses to feel a sense of belonging and connection with the natural world. Heightened awareness in the forest can enrich your daily life.

5. Exercise: Fitness doesn't always require structured workouts. Forest walks provide an opportunity for physical activity that's free and enjoyable.

6. Improved Sleep: Regular walks in nature have been shown to positively impact sleep quality. Embracing nature's tranquility can lead to better rest at night.

Understanding Phytoncides

Phytoncides are natural oils released by trees and plants, known for their woody scent. Research suggests that phytoncides offer various benefits, such as boosting immune function and reducing feelings of depression and anxiety.

While scientists continue to explore the effects of traditional medications on mental health, many experts emphasize the healing power of nature.

Spending time in the woods can't replace medical advice, but it can complement a healthy lifestyle. If aimless wandering isn't suitable for you, consider learning about forest bathing techniques.

Getting Ready for a Hike

Excited to explore nature? Interested in finding nearby forest bathing spots? Here's how to prepare for a fulfilling hike:

1. Find the Right Trail: Check out national, state, and local parks for suitable hiking trails. You're likely to discover a few scenic paths to explore.

2. Comfortable Gear: Ensure you're dressed comfortably for the hike. Wear sturdy boots or shoes, comfortable pants, and bring along a water bottle to stay hydrated.

3. Navigation Tools: Take a map of the hiking trails or the entire forest. This helps you navigate and explore without getting lost.

4. Backpack: Use a hiking backpack to carry any essentials or personal items you might need during your adventure.

Forest Baths: Frequently Asked Questions

What is a forest bath?

A forest bath involves immersing oneself completely in nature, particularly under the shelter of trees, to connect deeply with the environment and experience inner peace.

What is forest bathing called in Japanese?

In Japanese, forest bathing is known as "shinrin yoku."

Do I need any special equipment?

Depending on the duration and location of your forest bath, you might need some camping essentials, such as:

- Comfortable and waterproof hiking boots or shoes

- A spacious and waterproof hiking backpack

- Moisture-wicking hiking trousers with pockets

- Hiking poles or stability poles

- A book about forest bathing (especially if you don't have an instructor)

Is forest bathing beneficial?

Yes, forest bathing offers numerous benefits for the mind, body, and soul. It reduces stress, enhances feelings of happiness, promotes relaxation, mindfulness, and fosters a deeper connection with nature.

Where does the forest bath originate?

Forest bathing, or shinrin-yoku, originated in Japan during the 1980s. Initially, it was introduced as part of government campaigns to counteract the negative effects of technology on Japanese citizens.

What is forest bathing certification?

Forest bathing is often incorporated into classes, rehabilitation programs, and wellness retreats. Certification ensures that instructors can effectively guide participants in maximizing the benefits of forest bathing, providing a solid foundation for those who wish to practice or teach the activity to others.

Chapter 10

My Grounding Experience

About a year ago, I decided to try grounding for myself. I got a kit that included a special sheet, wires, an outlet tester, and a metal rod. My house is old, so I used the tester to find only two outlets properly grounded. I plugged the sheet into one of them and stepped on it with my girlfriend. Right away, we felt a tingling sensation, especially in our hands. Putting the sheet on our bed, we slept better and felt more rested, though I struggled a bit waking up in the mornings.

I don't have chronic inflammation, so I didn't notice any changes there. But my sleep did improve noticeably.

I've been using the grounding kit on and off since then, not noticing much until recently. I read that a direct connection to the Earth might work better. So, a few days ago, I connected the sheet to a metal rod planted in my backyard. The tingling sensation and deep sleep effect were even stronger this time.

Grounding for Everyone

Grounding yourself to the Earth can bring benefits to anyone, especially those dealing with chronic inflammatory diseases. While a grounding set with cables can be a bit pricey, around $200, it might be worth it.

This method requires minimal effort – just sleep while in contact with it, and you're connected to the Earth's free electrons.

For daytime use, there are smaller grounding mats that can be placed in front of the TV or computer, protecting you from harmful electromagnetic waves.

Recap: How to Ground Yourself

Grounding techniques offer various health benefits by increasing your body awareness. Earthing, in particular, reconnects you with the Earth and has been shown to reduce inflammation by neutralizing free radicals.

These techniques help:
- Clear your mind,
- Recharge your energy, and
- Calm your emotions.

By practicing grounding exercises, you can enhance your mental and physical performance, as well as your overall well-being. Walking barefoot on the Earth is a calming and enjoyable experience that brings you closer to yourself.

Enjoy!

Made in the USA
Coppell, TX
29 September 2024